There Was a Time

There Was a Time

THE STORY OF EVOLUTION

by Suzanne Stark Morrow
illustrated by Enrico Arno

E. P. DUTTON & CO., INC.
NEW YORK

To Margaret, Mark, and Jefferson

FIRST EDITION

Published simultaneously in Canada by Clarke, Irwin & Company Limited, Toronto and Vancouver.

Library of Congress Catalog Card Number: 65-21291

There was a time when
man got along without
    electric lights,
    cars,
    houses,
    clothes,
    and stoves.

There was a time when
man got along without
    cows,
    sheep,
    chickens,
    and dogs.

There was a time when
man got along without
    books,
    paper,
    pencils,
    and words.

There was a time when
there was not even man.

Many millions of years ago, there was nothing on this earth but water and land.

The sun warmed the chemicals in the water, and one day living cells appeared.

For thousands of years, the cells drifted about in the water, sloshed on the muddy banks, or lay quietly on the bottom of the lakes.

Gradually the cells grew bigger. Some divided to become two cells. They divided again and again. Larger plants and animals were formed.

To move through the water for food, some cells formed a tail. Other cells became a head.

Many of the fish thus formed found themselves in dark, muddy water. They had to find a new way to breathe. Gradually they grew air chambers in their heads and were then able to breathe both water and air.

Time went on. Much of the water evaporated. Plants and animals were all over one another—struggling and floundering to stay alive.

Some plants were squeezed out of the salty water and onto the muddy banks. They found a strange world of air, and in order to live they had to change. They grew in new ways, and as time passed, they became shrubs and trees.

The fish left the crowded water, too. In their struggle to stay alive their air chambers were gradually replaced by lungs. The animals then breathed as easily on land as in water. They used their fins to go from place to place, and after millions of years these fins developed into legs.

The first land animals had legs that spread out from their sides. They had to waddle along the ground.

As animals moved more and more on land, their legs gradually changed. Their legs began to grow straight under them, and they could now move faster in search of food.

11

In order to stay alive, the animals on land had to grow in other ways, too.

One animal grew a hard shell to keep his body from drying up in the sun.

Others grew fur. These were the first mammals. They were animals about the size of rats, with furry bodies and pointed noses.

And another grew a thick, horny skin.

Some reptiles liked to eat as much food as they could find. They grew to be eighty feet long, and thundered over the earth gobbling down bushes and branches.

But some reptiles didn't like to eat vegetables. They grew strong legs and sharp teeth in order to catch and eat the other animals.

Other reptiles grew wings, and took to the trees for safety.
All reptiles didn't look alike, but they acted alike in one
way. They didn't take care of their children. When the eggs
hatched, the young came out of their shells and had to start
looking for food from the day they were born.

The timid mammals grew, too.

These mothers took care of their young until they were old enough to look after themselves.

This was a warm, busy earth, alive with birds and snakes. Then earthquakes shook the ground, and volcanoes erupted.

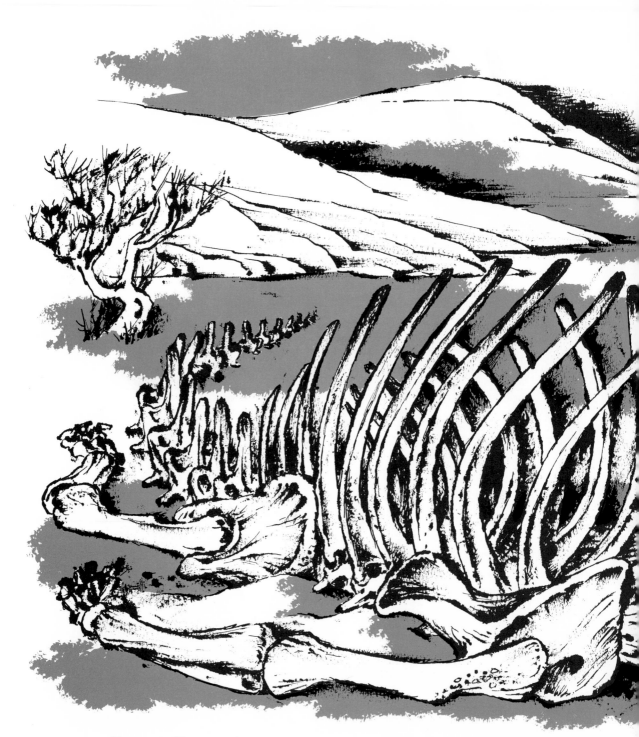

Over millions of years the warm swamplands became covered with ice and snow.

Many of the reptiles were too big to get away to find food elsewhere. Most of them died.

The mammals were able to run on to new pastures to hunt for food. They found trees and grass and wild flowers growing everywhere.

Not all the mammals liked to eat grass. Some wanted meat. These animals grew claws and sharp teeth, and prowled the forests looking for other animals to eat.

To protect themselves, the grass-eating mammals had to change, too.

Some grew horns and tusks.

Other animals learned to dig holes in the ground, and hide.

Another kind learned to scurry up the trees.

And still a different animal learned to swing high in the tree branches.

Again the climate changed. The wet, grassy forest lands gradually became dry and dusty. Most of the trees died, and nothing was left but flat open plains dotted here and there with a tree.

The tree-swinging animals had to run across open spaces to look for food. They couldn't move fast enough or far enough on all four legs, and many died.

Others tried something new. They stood straight up on their hind legs and discovered they could travel long distances to look for food. They didn't use their front legs to go from place to place. They used them to help get food.

The animals could pick up sticks, and as they pushed the sticks into the earth they discovered that roots could be pried up.

When the animal struck the stick against a high tree branch, nuts fell down. He liked berries, nuts, and roots best; but because there was little rain, the ground was often bare and brown. He had to eat whatever he could find and catch: mice, turtles, grubs. He shared what he had with his family. They lived by themselves.

He found he could throw a stone. Sometimes the stone
hit the ground, and chipped. Sometimes the stone killed a
rabbit. But when he tried to eat the rabbit, his teeth weren't
sharp enough to tear the fur and skin. He picked up a rock
and hit it against another rock. As he watched the edge
chip, he also thought about what he was doing. With the
rock—now sharp as a knife—he skinned the rabbit and ate
the meat. He had sharpened this rock so he could eat, and
he saved it to use another time. He had made the first tool,
a stone chopper. He was thinking—and so there was man.

The first men liked being together, but they knew no words. They communicated with one another by making sounds. People lived like this for many thousands of years, until rabbits, squirrels, and other small animals became hard to find.

For food, people looked to the wild boars, oxen, baboons, and elephants that charged in herds over the land.

Only the man who could think of a way to kill these animals could stay alive.

A man tied a long strip of animal hide around a stone. He made three of these and tied them together at the end.

He held the tied end of the strips in his hand and swung the stones around and above his head. Other men crouched in the bushes, ready to attack with sticks the minute the animal fell.

He aimed at the feet of the running animal, and let go.
The stones flew through the air. They swirled around the
animal's feet, and the strips of hide wound around his legs.
Men ran from every direction to pounce on the fallen
animal.

The killing of a big animal took teamwork. And teamwork meant that men had to talk to and understand each other. The sounds these men made became words.

Man had to use his brain to find ways to stay alive. His brain, therefore, grew, and became strong. Now man could think of more ways to make his life easier.

He made a windbreak, which was the first house.

Then man thought to make clothes out of animal skin to keep warm in cold weather.

And, finally, one day fire was captured.

When lightning struck and trees blazed with fire, most animals and men ran in terror. But one brave man walked close, broke a branch from a tree, and carried fire back to his camp.

With better weapons and ways to keep warm, men didn't have to spend all their time working to stay alive. They had time to think of other things.

They thought about making themselves look more attractive. They punched holes in shells and animal teeth and strung them on strips of hide to hang around their necks. They put feathers in their hair. From the ground, they took white pipe clay and red ocher and painted designs on their faces, chests, and arms.

They were now able to take more of what was around
them and make it into what they wanted.

They drew pictures of the animals they hunted. They believed this gave them a magic power over the animals. They thought that capturing an animal in a painting would help them capture it in hunting.

Man thought about everything more and more, and he felt strong.

And then man began to plant grain, to tame animals, to weave cloth.

Man learned to write, to read, to make numbers, and on and on and on.

This is the way man grew, and this is the way man grows.